Chipper Cloud

George M. Davison

DORRANCE PUBLISHING CO., INC.
PITTSBURGH, PENNSYLVANIA 15222

Dorrance Publishing Co., Inc.
701 Smithfield Street
Pittsburgh, PA 15222
Visit our website at *www.dorrancebookstore.com*

ISBN: 978-1-4809-9773-8
eISBN: 978-1-4809-9774-5

"What a beautiful day! So many ways to be creative!
Let's see, where shall I start?" said Chipper.

"Should I drop a little rain on that garden?
Inspire some flowers to pop out of the ground?"

2

"Should I glide over that artist to
spark her imagination for a painting?"

3

"Oh! Kids! I love kids!
They're so creative!"

4

"Maybe I should make myself
into Inventalot Castle…or maybe a heart,
or a T. Rex. I bet they'd love that," said Chipper.

"Hey, Chipper," said Gizmo the eagle.
"Hey, Gizmo! Have you ever seen such a beautiful day?"
"I know, I know. Everybody's outside
watching me do barrel rolls and loop-the-loops!"

"Hey, let's play! What if I became a giant airliner,
and we could rule the skies together," said Chipper.
"You'd never be as fast as I am!" said Gizmo.

"Whoa!" shouted Gizmo.
"I'll never be as fast but I can make myself
one hundred times as big! ANYTHING is possible!"

"Owwwww!"
shouted Chipper.

10

"Anything is possible, eh, Chipper?"
snickered Stormy.

"Well...," gasped Chipper.

"What a bunch of BUNK! Why do anything?
It's not worth it," said Stormy.

"See, it's all pointless.
Why bother creating anything?" said Stormy.

14

"Because it's FUN! Nothing can stop my creativity,"
said a chipper Chipper.

"Oh, yeah? Anything you make, I can wreck.
Give up. It's hopeless."

"Hopeless? I LOVE creating," said Chipper. "And look!
My creativity inspires everyone else to be creative."

17

"Give up. I'll always be there to rain on their parade."

"And when you're done raining,
I'll be there making RAINBOWS."

"Oh, yeah?
Then I'll come back and storm some more."
20

"Good. We need those storms. The more rain,
the more flowers," said Chipper.

"The more flowers,
the more creative inspiration for artists."

"The more creativity,
the more beauty in the world."

"Oh, yeah?
Well, what if I NEVER STOP raining?"

24

"Then you've got FLOODS that wash everything away.
How 'bout that?" flashed Stormy.

"Stormy, there's NOTHING you can do
that can stop the positive power of creativity
to make something beautiful."

"Oh, yeah? What if I rained for a hundred years?
A thousand years? For...for...TWO BILLION YEARS?"

"Then you know what would happen?"

"I would destroy EVERYTHING!"

"No. Wrong. Just the opposite."

"What?!?"

"Two billion years of rain and rivers and floods
produced the Grand Canyon,
an astonishing Wonder of the World...

...and a place that continues to inspire artists and photographers from around the world!"

"But...but...."
"Right," said Chipper.

34

"I don't understand you," said Stormy.

"No, that's not true. The truth is...
you don't understand yourself."

"What?!?"

"Think about it, Stormy. No matter what you do,
you create rainbows and flowers and natural wonders."

38

"Well...."

"What is a cloud? Just water—
the key element for all life on earth—in the air!
You know what that means?" said Chipper.

"What?"

"Clouds like me—like US, my friend—we get to be everywhere at once! We're in the air! We're the CREATIVE INSPIRATION around every great inventor, every artist, everyone who makes things and does things and builds things!" said Chipper.

"Take me, for example. I was there
when Edison invented the light bulb!"

"I was there when Van Gogh painted those amazing sunflowers! (And, oh, by the way, your rain helped grow them!)"

44

"I'm there for anyone who wants a flash of inspiration and a jolt of creative energy to bring something new and wonderful for the world," said Chipper.

"Boy. You've really taken the fun
out of being Stormy...."

"You want to have some REAL fun?
Then be who you really are."

47

"I'm Stormy, the dark cloud
that rains on everyone's parade."

"Not anymore. Now you're BRAINSTORM,
the electric charge that creates BREAKTHROUGHS
wherever you go!" said Chipper.

"Brainstorm? Me? Hmmmm…you really think…."

"The two of us, we were put here
for the same purpose: to be creative," said Chipper.

"To make flowers...."

"And rainbows?" asked Stormy.
"Yes, and rainbows, Stormy," said Chipper.

"And to inspire people to look up into the sky and say,
'Hey! That looks like....'"
"A wizard's hat," exclaimed Stormy.
"Now you've got it, Stormy," said Chipper.

"A pirate ship, a locomotive, a football, a flying saucer!" said a fun-filled Stormy.

"Way to go! You've got the secret to creativity!
Create for the JOY of it!" said Chipper.

"But...but what if I forget and
go back to the way I was?"

"Don't worry. I'll be right here to remind you,"
said Chipper. "You were born to create great things
with passion and joy. Just smile, open your heart,
and let it flow into the world."